Interesting Facts and Sports Stories

Basketball – Part 1

ErikBruning

ISBN: 9798642409992

DEDICATION

For the real sports fan this is a must-read book. It is perhaps the biggest collection of facts and what some might call fiction, since some of the sports stories have been passed on for generations. Although it focuses on baseball, there are scores of insightful anecdotes that crossover into many other sports. It doesn't stop there. It shows how intertwined with everyday life baseball has been over the years, from its relationship to world conflicts to the impact on US Presidents.

CONTENTS

Chapter 3 – Here comes the 1980s White Lines

Introduction

If you're a fan of basketball, you're in the right place. This book is chock-full of stats, tidbits and sometimes irreverent facts about your favorite NBA teams and players. This book could settle some arguments among your friends about who's the better player. This book could win you a drink at a bar when you pull out the random nugget of information to settle that bet.

This book will have some of the lesser-known back stories about those players and teams that everyone knows about. You'll learn about players who got along, and teammates who didn't. The quips and quotes of famous hoopsters, and hopefully, maybe some new perspectives of players from different eras throughout the history of the NBA.

Chapter 1 – Back in the Day

While it's easy to make fun of all that grainy black-and-white footage, what looks like sped-up film and unorthodox shooting styles, there were plenty of reasons the NBA of yesteryear was just as interesting as today's global brand as we know it. There were innovations, star players, dynastic teams, and a little bit of controversy along the way.

The Birth of a League

The NBA as everyone knows it today is far different than its first day of existence on Aug. 3, 1949. The National Basketball Association was actually the merger of two rival leagues, the Basketball Associated of America (BAA) and the National Basketball League (NBL).

The NBL was created in the mid-1930s, but known as the Midwest Basketball Conference. In 1937, it was changed to the National Basketball League. Corporate sponsorship took on a much bigger role in those days as Goodyear, Firestone and General Electric – the original owner of NBC – created the league.

What was originally an informal 10-game season among teams in Midwest cities grew quickly in popularity. The home team could choose the format of either playing in four 10-minute quarters or three 15-minute periods.

The NBL was unopposed until 1946, when the BAA originated. The big selling points for the BAA were they played in large cities, played 48 minutes instead of 40, allowed players a sixth foul and acquired players directly from college.

Both leagues were at risk financially trying to run the other out of business, but in 1949, representatives from both leagues met in New York City at the Empire State Building. There, they agreed to merge together to form the National Basketball Association as a 17-team league under BAA president Maurice Podoloff.

Maurice Podoloff

Podoloff himself is a unique character in sports history because he is the only man to run two professional sports simultaneously. He was also the president of the American Hockey League. Podoloff, though, is more widely known in basketball circles since the NBA's Most Valuable Player is awarded the Maurice Podoloff Trophy at season's end.

Podoloff served as NBA commissioner until 1963, and the native of Ukraine was inducted into the Basketball Hall of Fame in 1974. The man in charge of some of the world's tallest athletes was himself only 5-foot-2.

Danny Biasone and Leo Ferris

If Podoloff is to be given credit for running the NBA, Biasone and Ferris are the ones who arguably saved the league from extinction in the mid-1950s. Biasone was the owner of the Syracuse Nationals (today's Philadelphia 76ers), one of the original teams of the NBL and one of the seven teams that were absorbed into the NBA at the time of the merger.

The league struggled to make headway in the late 1940s, and by the early 1950s, it had contracted to eight teams. The slow pace of play and foul-filled contests after one team raced out to a huge lead turned off many fans, leaving the league in limbo. In the 1950-51 season, the Fort Wayne Pistons defeated the Minneapolis Lakes 19-18, and the teams combined for just four fourth-quarter points.

Biasone and Nationals general manager Leo Ferris tried out their idea for a shot clock during a scrimmage in 1954. Biasone felt an entertaining game in his view was when the teams combined to attempt approximately 120 shots. Ferris took the number of seconds (2,880) in a game, divided by 120, and that's how the 24-second shot clock was born.

George Mikan

George Mikan was one of the primary reasons Biasone devised the shot clock to speed up the game. Mikan, who averaged at least 20.6 points in each of his four NBA seasons as well as 13.5 rebounds per game the first four years the league tracked rebounds as a statistic, was a 6-foot-10, 245-pound giant who dominated in the paint on both ends of the court.

He used his long reach to shoot over smaller players and to block shots defensively, essentially serving as a one-man wall around the basket. In fact, Mikan was so good at blocking shots that the NBA had to create what is now known as the "goaltending rule" in which a player cannot block a shot while the ball is on its way down.

Offensively, Mikan had the rarest of skills, the ability score from close range using either hand. Anyone who has ever tried out for a high school basketball team at some point in their lives has done the "Mikan Drill," in which a player shoot layups, alternating with each hand, and using the basket as a shield while not letting the rebound touch the floor.

Mikan's Lakers won four of the first five NBA titles in league history and also set a precedent for the league's penchant of having dynasties that continues to this day.

Red Auerbach

Forever associated with the Boston Celtics and his trademark victory cigars after winning a grand total of 16 titles as coach, general manager or president of the team, Auerbach got his start further south on the East Coast with the Washington Capitols in the BAA. He made the playoffs all three years there, but failed to win a title.

Auerbach also had a one-season stint with the Tri-Cities Blackhawks in the NBA's inaugural 1949-50 season. He went 28-29 and resigned after owner Ben Kerner traded away John Mahnken, whom Auerbach considered his best player.

Auerbach was hired by the Celtics mainly because then-owner Walter Brown asked for recommendations from the local media, and they suggested him. Auerbach is also credited with breaking down the NBA's racial barrier by selecting Chuck Cooper in the second round of the 1950 draft. Cooper was the first African-American to be selected by an NBA team, and by 2015, almost three of every four players in the NBA (74.4 percent) were African-American – the highest of any major professional sports leagues in the U.S. and Canada. Auerbach is also credited with being the first coach to have a starting five of all African-Americans, beginning a game with Bill Russell, Willie Nauls, Tom Sanders, Sam Jones and K.C. Jones in 1964. He also made Russell the first African-American coach in North American pro sports when he tabbed the center as a player-coach for the 1967-68 season.

Bob Cousy

Auerbach was the architect of the second dynasty of the NBA, but one that lasted far longer with nine titles in a 10-year span. While almost everyone can tick off the names of the Celtics stars – Cousy, Sharman, Russell, Sanders, Havlicek, Heinsohn, Ramsay and Jones – Auerbach wasn't sold on Cousy at first.

Many expected Cousy to be Auerbach's first pick in the 1950 draft, but he wanted no part of the point guard who led Boston-area school Holy Cross to the 1947 NCAA Tournament title. Auerbach opted for center Charlie Share with the No. 1 overall pick and famously asked the local media, "Am I supposed to win, or please the local yokels?" in defending his selection.

Cousy went third to the Tri-Cities Blackhawks, but he did not report because he was trying to get a driving school off the ground in Worcester, Massachusetts, and had no desire to relocate to that part of the Midwest. The Chicago Stags – the city's precursor to the Chicago Bulls – acquired his draft rights in a trade, but the team folded before the 1950-51 season after just four years in existence.

Cousy was awarded to Boston in a dispersal draft, but the flashy style.

Auerbach originally had no use for became viable because Cousy could quickly move the ball in a loaded Celtics offense that included Hall of Famers Ed Macauley and Bill Sharman. The trio would revolutionize the NBA further through fast-break basketball and create the foundation for what is the best dynasty in league history.

Bill Russell

The Celtics' dynasty didn't really begin until Auerbach acquired Russell after the St. Louis Hawks selected him No. 2 in the 1956 draft. The deal almost never came to fruition, though, because after originally agreeing to send Ed Macauley to St. Louis for the rights to Russell, Hawks owner Ben Kerner wanted more.

Kerner and Auerbach had a contentious history – Auerbach resigned after one season in Tri-Cities following a trade Kerner made without Auerbach's knowledge, and the Celtics also had Kerner's former top pick Bob Cousy after the guard refused to sign with the team when it was located in Tri-Cities. To complete the Russell trade, Kerner wanted Cliff Hagan, picked by the Celtics in 1953 who had yet to play because he was drafted into the military.

Auerbach signed off the deal and acquired Russell, and later selected his San Francisco teammate K.C. Jones and Tommy Heinsohn that year. Though Russell did not join the team until midseason because he was also part of the 1956 U.S. Olympic team, he more than made up for that lost time as he averaged 14.7 points and a league-high 19.6 rebounds in leading the Celtics to their first NBA title.

It was the beginning of an incredible career that resulted in 11 NBA titles over 13 seasons as a player and coach that also included five MVP awards – only Michael Jordan has more. Additionally, in 2009, the

NBA announced it was going to name the NBA Finals MVP Award after Russell.

Tom Heinsohn

These days, Heinsohn is still the beloved Celtics television announcer who gives out "Tommy Points" for hustle and clutch plays, but Heinsohn holds a unique spot in the team's history. He is the only person that was with the Celtics in some official capacity – player, coach or otherwise – for all 17 of their NBA titles and all 21 NBA Finals appearances.

While Heinsohn and Bill Russell were good teammates, they were not – and still are not – particularly close. Russell felt he deserved the 1957 NBA Rookie of the Year award more than Heinsohn and told him publicly he deserved half of the $300 bonus that came with the award. Heinsohn also made an autograph request of Russell for a family member the center never fulfilled. The two simply had a pure basketball working relationship and little else.

By the time Heinsohn's playing career ended in 1965, Auerbach wanted him to take the Celtics coaching reins. But Heinsohn refused because he felt he wouldn't be able to control Russell given the lack of a relationship between the two. It was Heinsohn who suggested to Auerbach he make Russell player-coach given how the center had the basketball acumen to do both roles.

Heinsohn eventually took the Celtics' coaching job three seasons later, after Russell retired, and led Boston to the 1973-74 title.

Bob Pettit

Despite their dynasty, the Celtics did not own a monopoly on the NBA's greatest players. Bob Pettit was one of those stars, with a basketball start that harkens another of the game's greats – Micahel Jordan.

Pettit grew up in Louisiana, where he was cut from his high school's varsity teams both his freshman and sophomore years. But a five-inch growth spurt, coupled with a work ethic his father helped instill, Pettit led his high school to a state title as a junior.

After a standout career at LSU in which he was a two-time All-American, he was the second overall pick in the 1954 draft by the Milwaukee Hawks, yet another stop in the nomadic franchise's history. Pettit's $11,000 salary was the highest by an NBA draft pick at the time.

Berner realized Pettit was too small to be a center in the NBA and moved him to forward. His speed at the position, which he used to be one of the best offensive rebounders in league history, resulted in a standout 11-year career in which he averaged 26.4 points and 16.2 rebounds and the 1958 NBA title over the Celtics.

Pettit scored a playoff-record 50 points in that series-clinching victory, which is the only reason why the Celtics did not reel off 10 straight titles from 1957-66 and why the Hawks reached the NBA finals four times in a five-year span from 1957-61.

Wilt Chamberlain

One can't talk about Bill Russell without Wilt Chamberlain, they are the yin and the yang of the early NBA and pioneers along with George Mikan at the center position. And Chamberlain was everything Russell was not when you consider the statistical superlatives he achieved while being denied an NBA title until later in his career.

The Philadelphia Warriors were actually Chamberlain's second professional team. His first was the Harlem Globetrotters, with whom he played from 1958-59. The NBA did not accept players into the draft before the completion of the graduating class, and Chamberlain had no interest in returning to Kansas following an inconsistent junior season. So he signed a $50,000 contract with the Globetrotters, with the highlight of his year barnstorming a meeting with then-Russian prime minister Nikita Khrushchev.

Chamberlain broke eight NBA records his rookie season and was the first player in league history to be named NBA MVP and Rookie of the Year in the same season. Only Wes Unseld equaled that feat in 1969. It took Chamberlain all of 56 games to set the single-season points record and he finished his rookie season averaging 37.6 points and 27.0 rebounds.

Chamberlain's career shooting percentage (54.0 percent) was better than his free throw percent (51.1). In the 1966-67 season, when he won his first NBA title, the difference was a career-high 24.2 percent as he shot 68.3 percent from the floor and 44.1 percent from the line.

RANDOM FACTS AND FIGURES

1. During their dynasty of 11 titles in 13 years, the Celtics averaged 55.07 wins as the length of the NBA season went from 72 games to 75 (1959-60) to 79 (1960-61) to 80 (1961-62) to 81 (1966-67) to the current 82-game format (1967-68). Only once, during their last title-winning season in 1968-69, did the Celtics have a winning percentage of less than 600.

2. It took the Hawks' franchise nine years to have as many playoff series wins as city locations (3 – Tri-Cities, Milwaukee, Atlanta).

3. How important was the introduction of the 24-second shot clock? Teams combined to average 79 points in the 1953-54 season, the last one before it was introduced. In 1954-55, that number jumped to 93 points. By 1957, the figured jumped another 14 points to 107.

4. Despite his offensive prowess via his ambidextrous ways around the basket, George Mikan was a career 40.4 percent shooter from the field. He did, however, shoot 78.2 percent from the foul line.

5. How much did Red Auerbach and Ben Kerner dislike each other? In the 1957 NBA Finals,

Auerbach was fined $300 for punching Kerner in Game 3.

6. Bill Russell's defense was so good the Celtics jokingly referred to it as the "Hey, Bill!" defense because it would often take place when a defender got beat and would yell to Russell to rotate over to help and use his height to affect the shot.

7. Bob Cousy never shot 40 percent from the field in a season despite averaging almost 18 attempts per game. But he did lead the NBA in assists for eight straight seasons from 1952-60.

8. One of the reasons Bill Russell lasted until the No. 2 pick was because of the Ice Capades. Celtics owner Walter Brown was also president of the Ice Capades and he promised Rochester Royals owner Lee Harrison, whose team held to the No. 1 pick, that he would send the Ice Capades to Rochester for a show if they didn't select Russell.

9. Dolph Schayes, who won the 1955 NBA title with the Syracuse Nationals, averaged a double-double in points and rebounds every season throughout the 1950s.

10. There were 17 teams when the NBA played its first season in

11. 1949-50. The second season started with just 11 after three teams left for the ill-fated National Professional Basketball League and three teams folded. A seventh team, the Washington Capitols, folded 35 games into the season.

12. The Eastern Division in the 1952-53 season was incredibly top-heavy. New York, Syracuse and Boston were separated by 1 ½ games as they combined for 140 wins. The other two teams – Baltimore and Philadelphia – were a cumulative 28-111 while going 2-47 on the road.

13. Maurice Stokes could have been one of the best players in NBA history had he not suffered a seizure on the team's flight from Detroit to Cincinnati following a playoff game in 1958. In his three seasons, Stokes averaged 16.4 points and 17.3 rebounds.

14. Wilt Chamberlain actually took a pay cut with his first NBA deal. After making $50,000 for his one season with the Harlem Globetrotters, he made $30,000 in his first season with the Philadelphia Warriors, who made him the highest-paid player in the league with that deal.

15. Like George Mikan before him, Chamberlain was so dominant offensively he forced NBA rules changes. While the more well-known one was the widening of the lane, the league also banned him

from making free throws by dunking. Yes, Chamberlain was so long and so athletic he was able to dunk from the foul line without a running start.

16. At their absolute best, the Celtics averaged a club-record 124.5 points in the 1959-60 season. Five players – Tom Heinsohn, Bob Cousy, Bill Sharman, Bill Russell and Frank Ramsay – all scored more than 1,000 points that season. It's the fourth-highest average in NBA history, eclipsed only by two of Wilt Chamberlain's teams (1961-62 and 1966-67) and the 1981-82 Denver Nuggets, who averaged 126.5 points… and gave up 126.0 per game.

TRIVIA TIME

1. How many times did the Celtics beat the Hawks to win the NBA Finals during their 13-year dynasty?

    A. 1
    B. 2
    C. 3
    D. 4

2. How many times was Tommy Heinsohn elected to the NBA All-Star Game?

    A. 1
    B. 2
    C. 3
    D. 4

3. From 1959-1960 to 1967-78, Bill Russell and Wilt Chamberlain won all but one NBA MVP award. Who won the one they didn't?

    A. Oscar Robertson
    B. Tom Heinsohn
    C. Bob Cousy
    D. Bob Pettit

4. What was George Mikan's highest single-season scoring average?

    A.   31.4
    B.   27.6
    C.   28.0
    D.   28.4

5. Which of these players DID NOT average 30 points per game in at least two seasons prior to 1970?

    A.   Elgin Baylor
    B.   Oscar Robertson
    C.   Jerry West
    D.   Rick Barry

Answers:

1 – C

2 – B

3 – A

4 – D

5 –D.

CHAPTER 2 – The American Basketball Association (ABA)

Even with an established dynasty in the Boston Celtics and a parade of stars in Cousy, Heinsohn, Russell and Chamberlain, there were still plenty of people ready to challenge the National Basketball Association as the top league for hoops in the country. After all, unlike its football, baseball and hockey counterparts, the NBA was still a relatively young league – it was heading towards early adulthood as the 1970s approached.

Having fended off the fledgling American Basketball League in the early 1960s; the league had only one full season in 1961-62 and folded during the 1962-63 season, the NBA had the game to itself for five seasons before the next rival league would take form. That would be the American Basketball Association, whose legacy continues today in the NBA.

A Grand Plan

The owners of the 11 teams that comprised the ABA didn't have breaking up the NBA as a goal. To the contrary, their end game was to join the more established league. That was a selling point to potential owners as the league was formed, that it would be cheaper to form a rival league than pay the league an expansion fee as a new NBA franchise.

What the ABA lacked in terms of established publicity, it aggressively sought with its distinctive on-court aesthetics. Start with the ball, which was red, white and blue as opposed to the NBA's orange. It opted for a 30-second shot clock in comparison to the NBA's 24-second one. But the ABA's lasting legacy is making the 3-point line part of basketball at every level, though it was something the ABL utilized in its brief existence.

Chaos at the Top

While the ABA's first commissioner was former NBA great George Mikan, who introduced both the 3-point line and multi-colored basketball, he wound up being one of seven commissioners in the league's nine years of existence.

Mikan served as commissioner from 1967-69 before resigning and giving way to James Carson Gardner. His biggest claim to fame was moving the Houston Mavericks to North Carolina in 1969, with the Cougars playing in Charlotte shortly after he failed to secure a second term in the U.S. House of Representatives. In the end, it was another former NBA great, Dave DeBusschere, who took over as commissioner in 1975 and helped negotiate the deal that led to the ABA-NBA merger the following year.

Traveling Shoes

Nearly all 11 teams that took the court in 1967 for the ABA's inaugural season wound up making at least one move to a different city, state or region. In fact, only two teams _ the Indiana Pacers and Kentucky Colonels _ stayed in one place in league history. And of the 11, four were part of the 1976 merger with the NBA.

The Pacers were arguably the most successful ABA franchise, winning three titles and reaching the finals on two other occasions. They had three different MVPs in their title-winning campaigns, first swingman Roger Brown in 1970, then guard Freddie Lewis in 1972 and forward-center George McGinnis the following year.

The New York Nets were the only other team to win multiple ABA titles, doing so first in 1974 and again in the league's final season in 1976. The Kentucky Colonels reached the finals three times in a five-year span from 1971-75, finally breaking through for their only title in 1975 by denying the Pacers a fourth ABA crown.

The Colonels, who played at Freedom Hall in Louisville, also had the best single season in ABA history, going 68-16 in 1971-72 and winning the Eastern Division by a whopping 23 games over the Virginia Squires. Center Artis Gilmore, standing an imposing 7-foot-3, won Rookie of the Year and MVP honors by averaging 23.8 points, 17.8 rebounds and 5.0 blocks. He and Dan Issel formed a lethal tandem as Issel, a former collegiate standout down the road in Lexington at Kentucky, averaged 30.6 points and 11.2 rebounds.

But that team was bounced in six games in the divisional semifinals by the New York Nets. Kentucky lost the first two games at home by double-digit margins and never recovered, bowing out in six.

Franchise movement, save Indiana and Kentucky, was a defining hallmark of the ABA. While the Dallas Chaparrals stayed in-state and eventually became the San Antonio Spurs, the Houston Mavericks became the Carolina Cougars and then moved to St. Louis in 1974.

The Denver Nuggets franchise originally started in Kansas City, but never played a game there. They were also known as the Denver Larks, and then the Rockets before switching to the Nuggets in 1974. The ABA had a franchise in Florida, the Miami Floridians, that had its roots in Minnesota.

Will Ferrell's comedy movie "Semi-Pro" includes a fictional ABA team called the Flint Tropics that he was trying to include in the NBA merger, working out an agreement with the league's commissioner that the top four teams would be the ones that would go to the NBA. Former ABA stars Gilmore and George Gervin have cameo roles.

The ABA had two franchises in Minnesota in its brief history as the Muskies were there for the league's first season before bolting to Miami, and then the Pittsburgh Pipers set up a shot for one season before returning to western Pennsylvania for the 1969-70 season.

The Shrewd Spirit of St. Louis

By the time the Spirits arrived in St. Louis in 1974, it was the team's third city after previous stops in Houston (Mavericks) and Carolina (Cougars). The club was also on their second set of owners as James Gardner had bought the team from a group led by T.C. Morrow and had then-Houston Oilers owner Bud Adams as a minority partner.

The team spent two seasons in St. Louis, and was originally headed to a fourth city _ Salt Lake City _ to play in Utah before folding with the ABA-NBA merger. The Spirits and Kentucky Colonels each negotiated different buyouts with the NBA; Colonels owner John Y. Brown used his money to stay in basketball and bought the Buffalo Braves.

The Spirit ownership went a different route, folding the franchise and worked out an agreement in which they would receive a percentage of TV revenue from the four ABA teams joining the NBA in perpetuity. Over the next 38 years, this deal pocketed a cool $300 million for the ownership group. But that paled in comparison to the final payoff in which the ownership group agreed to a one-time, $500 million payout in 2014 in exchange for ending future payments.

Julius Erving

While the lack of a television contract ultimately led to the downfall of the ABA, it sure wasn't due to the lack of star power on the court. There were many players who were crossover stars in both leagues, including Issel, George Gervin, Connie Hawkins, Rick Barry and Gilmore, but none were more famous than a small forward from the University of Massachusetts. While he was named Julius Erving, he is better known as "Dr. J."

Erving led the ABA in scoring three times, once with the Virginia Squires and twice with the New York Nets. He is directly entwined with the fates of those two franchises, because once the Squires traded him following the 1972-73 season, they were never the same and eventually folded at the time of the merger.

The Nets, meanwhile, became one of the league's best teams and one of the four who would be taken into the NBA.

Erving spent only two seasons at the University of Massachusetts, where he averaged 26.3 points and 20.2 rebounds. He remains one of only six players to average at least 20 points and 20 rebounds in NCAA history.

Because he left after two seasons, the ABA was Erving's only option since NBA draft rules made no contingencies for players leaving college early. He signed with the Virginia Squires as a free agent and averaged 27.3 points as a rookie and helped them to the East Division finals.

Now eligible to enter the NBA draft, Erving somehow lasted until the 12th pick overall and was taken by the Milwaukee Bucks. One could only wonder what could have been had Erving signed with the Bucks and joined Oscar Robertson and Kareem Abdul-Jabbar. Erving instead signed with the Hawks before the draft because his former agent deceived him into signing a low-value contract.

There were three teams in two leagues vying for his services, and eventually, the U.S. court system had to intervene. Erving played three exhibition games with the Hawks before a three-judge panel ruled he belonged to the Squires. The NBA also fined the Hawks for signing him since the Bucks owned Erving's draft rights.

None of these distractions bothered Erving on the court as he averaged 31.9 points for the Squires. But the poor finances of the franchise forced them to trade Erving to the Nets before the 1973-74 season. With Erving leading the charge, the Nets won their first ABA title in 1974 and then the last ABA title two years later against the Nuggets. Erving averaged 34.7 points in that postseason and was in the top 10 of almost every category in the regular season.

George Gervin

The man was so cool he was known as "The Iceman." George Gervin didn't need those flashy dunks Erving made popular, he would simply glide to the basket and often finish with a finger roll or a layup. But before arriving in the ABA, Gervin had made an interesting name for himself in college.

He originally began at Long Beach State, where a young coach named Jerry Tarkanian was building a successful program. But Gervin, a Detroit native, was homesick and returned to Michigan before the end of the first semester. He would then enroll at Eastern Michigan and averaged 29.5 points in the 1971-72 season.

But he was far from being "The Iceman" at this point. In fact, he was the complete opposite. Gervin punched a player from Roanoke College in Eastern Michigan's College Division semifinals, earning himself a suspension and eventual removal from the team. His invites to the 1972 Olympic and Pan-Am Games teams were also rescinded, which leads one to wonder whether or not the U.S. team would have been in a position to be upset by the Soviet Union in the gold medal game had Gervin made the national squad.

Gervin came to the Squires by way of the Pontiac Chaparrals of the Eastern Basketball Association. It was another case of a star-crossed cameo as Squires scout and eventual Bulls and Suns head coach Johnny "Red" Kerr was responsible for bringing Gervin to the mid-Atlantic.

For one season, Gervin and Erving played together in the ABA, and the two would duel after practice. Gervin credited those games into making him a better player as his career arc began with one of the best players in the ABA in Erving and ended with one of the best in the NBA as he was teammates with a young Michael Jordan with the Bulls.

Dan Issel

After a standout career at Kentucky in which he set (and still holds) the school record with 2,138 points, Issel had a choice to make for his professional career. He was drafted in the eighth round by the Detroit Pistons in the 1970 NBA draft, or he could continue playing in the comforts of Kentucky after the Colonels made him the fourth overall pick.

Issel dominated the league throughout his six seasons, leading the league in scoring on three occasions. He teamed with 7-foot-2 center Artis Gilmore to form a devastating tandem as the Colonels won the 1975 ABA title. His reward for winning the title was being dealt to the Baltimore Claws, but since that team folded before the start of the 1975-76 season, he was then traded to Denver.

That started a highly successful 10-year run in which the Nuggets joined the NBA as part of the merger and became a perennial playoff contender in the 1980s under former ABA player Doug Moe. A seven-time All-Star, Issel finished his professional career with 27,482 points, which ranks 11th overall when combining points from both leagues. His 12,823 points in the ABA trail only fellow Kentucky alum and one-time teammate Louie Dampier.

Spencer Haywood

He may have been a one-year wonder in the ABA, but that was more than enough time for Haywood to make his case as one of the league's best players. Haywood set the precedent Erving followed by leaving college after two years – Haywood was the first "hardship case" who left school early after averaging 32.1 points and 21.5 rebounds for Detroit in the 1968-69 season – and signed with the Rockets, turning them into instant contenders.

Haywood averaged 30.0 points and 19.5 rebounds en route to being the league's Rookie of the Year and MVP in 1970. He was also the All-Star Game MVP after totaling 23 points, 19 rebounds and seven blocks for the West. Haywood would win an NBA title in 1980 with the Los Angeles Lakers, but he was also suspended for the final four games of the NBA Finals by coach Paul Westhead due to his struggles with a cocaine addiction.

The Squires' Sell-Off

Despite carrying the label of the Virginia Squires, the team never really had a home as it was one of the ABA's "regional" franchises. Home games were in one of four locations – Richmond, Hampton, Norfolk and Roanoke. And the Virginia area was the third stop for a franchise that originated in Oakland and moved to the nation's capital for the 1969-70 season.

Earl Foreman bought the team from singer Pat Boone and moved it to Washington. While the Squires was always considered one of the teams that were part of the

ABA-NBA merger when talks began in 1970, Bullets owner Abe Pollin was able to get the ABA owners to convince Foreman to move to Virginia to help the merger cause.

Foreman, though, constantly struggled with the team's finances and often had to jettison with star players. In 1970, he traded Rick Barry to the New York Nets for a draft pick and $200,000 to help balance the books. Despite dealing away the disgruntled superstar, the Squires won the East by 11 games.

The following year they drafted Erving and reached the second round of the semifinals. While Gervin and Erving were on the same team in the 1972-73 season, coach Al Bianchi rarely played them together until late in the season, and the Squires made a first-round exit at the hands of Kentucky.

Foreman sold Erving to the Nets prior to the 1973-74 season and then unloaded Gervin to the Spurs during the 1974 All-Star break. ABA commissioner Mike Storen tried to block the deal claiming it was not in the best interest of the league, but the deal went through as Gervin was sold for $225,000.

Those two deals doomed the franchise, which went a combined 30-137 the next two seasons. At one point, a player sued the team after a paycheck bounced. The Squires survived the 1975-76 season only because a local bank loaned Foreman $250,000. By May of 1976, the franchise was canceled by the league after it missed an assessment payment of $75,000. That meant the ownership group would receive no money from the impending merger.

A Coaches' Cradle

The difference in the rules, most notably the 3-point line, had a lasting effect on the game because some of the ABA's best guards would eventually become some of the NBA's best coaches. They included Larry Brown, whose own vagabond ways mirror the league he grew up with. Brown remains the only person to win an NCAA Tournament title and NBA title as a coach, and was elected to the Hall of Fame in 2002.

Hubie Brown led Kentucky to its only ABA title in 1975 and got his first NBA head coaching job with Atlanta two seasons later. A two-time NBA coach of the year, Hubie Brown is also a Hall of Famer with more than 500 wins to his credit.

Billy Cunningham was originally the fifth overall selection by the Philadelphia 76ers in the 1965 NBA draft, but he spent two seasons with the Carolina Cougars and was a fan favorite from his college playing days at North Carolina. Cunningham would then later coach the 76ers, and Erving, to the 1983 NBA title before his eventual induction into the Hall of Fame in 2006.

Doug Moe was an ABA journeyman player who averaged 16.3 points and 6.8 rebounds with four teams over five seasons in the league. After two assistant stints with Carolina and Denver in the ABA, he became the first NBA coach for San Antonio after the merger and got to the Western Conference finals in 1979.

Moe's up-tempo offense didn't have many set plays, it was predicated on quick passing and screens. He returned to Denver in 1980 and coached the Nuggets for 10 seasons, leading the league in scoring six times.

Random Facts and Figures

1. Only once in the ABA's nine years did its leading scorer average more points than the NBA's top scorer. In the 1968-69 season, Larry Jones averaged 28.4 points for the Denver Nuggets, edging out Elvin Hays' 28.38 mark for the San Diego Rockets.

2. Louie Dampier was one of the few players who not only spanned the ABA's entire nine-year existence but also one of just two players to play for only one team. The seven-time All-Star finished atop the league's scoring annals with 13,726 points despite never leading the ABA in scoring.

3. While many remember Rick Barry for his underhanded shooting style for free throws, he is the only player to lead the ABA, NBA and NCAA in scoring in a single season. He is also one of only four father-son duos to win NBA titles after his son Brent won the 2005 title with the San Antonio Spurs.

4. Erving finished fifth on the ABA's all-time scoring list with 11,662 points despite playing just five seasons in the league.

5. Issel is the only ABA player with two of the league's single-season top-five scoring totals. His league record of 2,538 points in the 1971-72 season would rank tied for 26th when combining the leagues.

6. Only 37 players made 100 or more 3-pointers in ABA history. By comparison, the shot is now so

entrenched in the NBA that 91 players hit 100 or more 3-pointers in the 2016-17 season alone.

7. The real reason it took nearly six years to complete the ABA-NBA merger was due to a lawsuit filed in 1970 by the NBA Players Association on behalf of Oscar Robertson that opposed the merger on antitrust grounds. The upshot of the lawsuit was that player salaries increased in both leagues before it was settled in 1976.

8. In the last three seasons before the mergers, teams from each league squared off in the preseason. The ABA won 62 of the 96 games, highlighted by the 1975 ABA champion Kentucky Colonels topping the NBA champion Golden State Warriors.

9. The ABA was forced to scrap its divisional format in the 1975-76 season because both the San Diego Sails and Utah Stars were forced to fold during the season due to financial difficulties.

10. The Chicago Bulls were one of the biggest opponents to the Colonels, being one of the four teams in the merger because they held the NBA draft rights to center Artis Gilmore. Colonels owner John Y. Brown folded the team for $3 million and eventually sold Gilmore's rights to the Bulls for another $1.1 million.

11. The Nets were unable to keep Erving because they had to pay an additional $4.8 million to the Knicks upon their entry into the NBA on top of the $3.2 million expansion fee the four newcomers had to pay. The Nets tried to sell Erving to the Knicks in

lieu of that fee, but the Knicks declined. Eventually, Erving went to the Philadelphia 76ers for $3 million.

12. Of the four teams who joined the NBA, the Spurs had the most immediate success with five division titles in their first six seasons. But it took until 1999 for them to become the first ABA team to win an NBA title.

13. After Gilmore went to the Bulls for $1.1 million for the first pick in the ABA dispersal draft, the next five players were selected from the Spirits of St. Louis for a combined $1.45 million.

14. According to Spurs owner Angelo Drossos, Celtics coach Red Auerbach was one of the most vocal opponents of the 3-point shot. That, of course, changed shortly after the Celtics drafted Larry Bird.

15. Moses Malone became the first player to bypass college and go straight to the pros when the Utah Stars selected him in the third round of the 1974 ABA draft.

TRIVIA TIME

1. Which of these teams did Larry Brown NOT serve as a head coach?

    A. The University of North Carolina
    B. San Antonio Spurs
    C. Detroit Pistons
    D. Kansas University

2. Who won the first slam dunk contest in 1976?

    A. David Thompson
    B. Larry Kenon
    C. Julius Erving
    D. Artis Gilmore

3. Who is the ABA's all-time leader in 3-point shooting percentage?

    A. Louie Dampier
    B. Darel Carrier
    C. Steve Jones
    D. Skeeter Swift

4. While Julius Erving is the only player to lead the ABA in scoring more than once, who set the all-time single-season scoring average at 34.6 points per game?

A. Rick Barry
B. Spencer Haywood
C. Dan Issel
D. Charlie Scott

5.   Which of these nicknames did NOT belong to the
      Memphis ABA franchise from 1970-75?

A. Sounds
B. Jazz
C. Pros
D. Tams

Answers:

1-A

2-C

3-B

4-D

5-B.

CHAPTER 3 – HERE COME THE 1980s

The 1980s marked the beginning of the NBA's rise in popularity, which began to take off after Magic Johnson and Larry Bird carried their one-time rivalry in college in the 1979 NCAA Tournament championship game to the pros with the two most established teams in the NBA – Johnson to the Los Angeles Lakers and Bird to the Boston Celtics.

But that was almost scuttled before it took off. After the NBA had survived an external challenge in the form of an ABA, it now had a growing problem from within. A cocaine epidemic was sweeping through the league, and no one was sure how to combat it.

White Lines

While Grandmaster Flash's rap song "White Lines" didn't hit the airwaves until nearly a generation later in 1996, there was plenty of cocaine to go around in the 1980s in the NBA. A joint article written for the Washington Post and Los Angeles Times in the summer of 1980 surveyed people "in the game" who estimated that between 40 and 75 percent of players were using cocaine and one out of every 10 players were "free basing."

It was the drug of choice in the NBA and it cut across all player levels and lines. Jazz forward Bernard King was arrested for possession and faced an additional charge of sodomy at the time of his arrest.

His teammate, Terry Furlow, died in a car accident. The autopsy revealed traces of cocaine and valium in his bloodstream.

At one point, Hawks president Stan Kasten estimated player use of cocaine at 75 percent, while team president Michael Gearon feared the league was

on the verge of an epidemic of free base." Free base was a more dangerous way to do cocaine, but it also caused a stronger addiction due to the intense high it provided.

A 2013 book "Larceny Games" written by Brian Tuohy made the claim the 1981-82 Knicks team could have been shaving points and fixing games in conjunction with a drug dealer. That team had Micheal Ray Richardson, a talented yet troubled guard who was suspended by the league three times for drug use before being given a permanent ban by the NBA in 1986. The ban lasted all of two seasons.

In the latter part of the 1986-87 season, three Phoenix Suns players were indicted on charges of drug trafficking, and a fourth – team star Walter Davis – was suspended after having a relapse in his battle with cocaine.

But the cautionary tale for the 1980s cocaine epidemic in the NBA was Len Bias. A talented forward at the University of Maryland, Bias was a two-time ACC Player of the Year and consensus first-team All-American in 1986. The Celtics selected him with the No. 2 overall pick that summer, with team president Red Auerbach having dreams of him and Larry Bird continuing Boston's dominance in the NBA.

But 48 hours after being selected, he returned to his dorm room and insufflated cocaine with friends and teammates in the overnight hours. He reportedly had a seizure and collapsed while talking with a friend. A 911 call made by a friend said Bias was "unconscious and not breathing." Less than three hours after that call, Bias was pronounced dead due to a cardiac arrhythmia related to the usage of cocaine.

The Celtics honored Bias with a memorial service, and the debate rages over whether or not Bias is the best player to never have played in the NBA.

Larry Legend Comes to Beantown Belatedly

Bird single-handedly carried little-known Indiana State to the NCAA title game in 1979. But even before that, the forward nicknamed "The Hick from French Lick" already had the NBA buzzing as one of its next potential stars.

Auerbach, the one-time Celtics coach responsible for their dynasty in the 1960s, had since moved into the front office and was determined to bring Bird to Boston. Auerbach was a master of scrutinizing every rule the league had and raised some eyebrows when he drafted Bird with the sixth pick in the 1978 draft.

Auerbach was legally allowed to do so since Bird was technically a member of the class of 1978. Many forget he started his collegiate career at Indiana, only to clash with Bobby Knight and leave Bloomington. It was after a short stint at Northwood Institute that he left for Terre

Haute and Indiana State.

Bird led the Sycamores to the 1978 NIT title, and with the Pacers holding the No. 1 pick that year, it made sense for Indiana to select the hometown hero.

But a meeting between Bird and Pacers GM Bob Leonard convinced the latter it might not be the best idea to draft Bird, who wanted to stay in college and could also demand a high salary if he did decide to come out and play in the pros. Eventually, Indiana traded the pick to Portland for the No. 3 selection and guard Johnny Davis.

And with Bird and the Sycamores going 33-0 before losing to Johnson and the Spartans, Auerbach looked like a genius yet again for his stashed draft pick.

Magic Casts a Spell in La-La Land

Their fates already entwined by the most-watched televised college basketball game, Earvin "Magic" Johnson did not have the same drama surrounding his lead-in to being drafted. The newly anointed NCAA Tournament champ was the first overall pick in the 1979 draft after averaging 17.1 points, 7.9 assists and 7.6 rebounds.

The 6-foot-9 Johnson revolutionized the point guard position because of his size and ball-handling skills. He could run the break, operate in the low post as a scorer, run a half-court offense and play some decent defense. No one since Oscar Robertson had the same skill-set as

Magic Johnson, and it would take until LeBron James to see it again.

Johnson had instant success in the NBA, helped in large part by the presence of Kareem Abdul-Jabbar. But it was in Abdul-Jabbar's absence in which Johnson started writing his legend as a pro. He filled in at center for the injured 7-foot-2 star and finished with 42 points, 15 rebounds and seven assists as the Lakers defeated Julius Erving and the Philadelphia 76ers 123-107 to win the NBA title.

A Skyline is Built in Houston

Size has long been coveted in the NBA, where a 7-footer can make a difference in a whole host of areas. But what if you had two 7-footers? Could you play them at the same time and not sacrifice speed against quicker teams? Could they co-exist on offense taking up that much space in the low post?

In 1983, the Rockets drafted 7-foot-4 Ralph Sampson, who had been a three-time All-American and three-time ACC Player of the Year at Virginia. Because there was still no NBA Draft lottery, the Rockets won the top overall pick by virtue of a coin flip. The year before, Sampson opted against entering the draft because the San Diego Clippers potentially could have won the No. 1 selection.

The Rockets made only marginal gains in Sampson's rookie season, more than doubling their win total while still finishing a horrid 29-53. Unlike Sampson,

Olajuwon was able to take a leap of faith on the draft coin flip since the options were Houston, where he played collegiately as part of the great "Phi Slamma Jamma" teams of Guy Lewis or Portland. The Rockets won the coin toss and made Olajuwon the No. 1 overall pick, two ahead of the Chicago Bulls, who selected a guard from North Carolina named Michael Jordan.

The two 7-footers instantly transformed the Rockets, making them instant contenders in the Western Conference. Olajuwon, a relentless learner who spent summers learning under the tutelage of one-time Rockets center Moses Malone, had the low-post finesse that perfectly complemented Sampson's classic back-to-the-basket game.

The Rockets improved another 19 games that year and made the playoffs, losing to the Jazz in the first round. But the 1985-86 season was one to remember as the Rockets won the Midwest Division and thrashed the Lakers in five games in the Western Conference finals. However, Bird and the 67-win Celtics were waiting in the finals and disposed of the Rockets in six games.

The "Twin Towers" experiment ended midway through the next season, when Sampson had a falling out with coach Bill Fitch and was traded to Golden State as part of a four-player deal.

Michael Jeffrey Jordan – The Early Years

Much has always been made about the fact Jordan "lasted" until the third overall pick in 1984, but Olajuwon created a Hall of Fame worthy career for himself while with the Rockets. And in the case of the Trail Blazers selecting Sam Bowie, well Jordan would have been a surplus of needs since they already had a pretty good shooting guard of their own in Clyde Drexler. Another Hall of Famer.

So Jordan essentially fell into the Bulls' laps at No. 3. But it still took some time for the greatest guard of his generation and arguably of all time to learn how to win. Remember, Jordan had no perimeter game early in his career. He averaged 28.2 points as a rookie while going just 9 for 52 from beyond the arc in the 1984-85 season.

That team finished 38-44 and was sent packing in the first round of the playoffs. He missed all but 18 games of his second season due to a foot.

injury, but served notice of his burgeoning star power when he averaged 43.7 points in a three-game sweep at the hands of the Celtics. His 63-point effort in a 135-131 double-overtime loss set a playoff scoring record that still stands.

Jordan's first winning season in Chicago did not come until the Bulls went 50-32 in 1987-88 and finished second to the Detroit Pistons, who would fluster him as he entered the prime of the first act of his career.

Motown's "Bad Boys"

Speaking of those Pistons, they supplanted the Celtics as the East's best team in the late 1980s after having gone through the rites of passage by being beat by the Celtics earlier in the decade. Coach Chuck Daly had assembled a strong nine-man rotation that featured stars in Isiah Thomas and Adrian Dantley as well as a rough-and-tumble frontcourt paced by Bill Laimbeer and a gangly youngster named Dennis Rodman.

While the nickname "Bad Boys" came about by way of a copy editor naming Detroit's 1987-88 season highlights tape with that title, the Pistons were a team that played fullcourt defense with gusto. Nothing was conceded, and disruption was the name of their game. Bumps were frequent, elbows were common and the swagger the Pistons carried was both hated and envied throughout the league. The Pistons nearly broke through in 1987, but lost in the conference finals to the Celtics in seven games as the home team won every time.

This was also the series that cemented the Pistons' "Bad Boys" persona as enraged Celtics center Robert Parrish suddenly pummeled Laimbeer late in Game 5. It turned out to be payback for a hard foul Laimbeer landed on Bird two games prior that almost started a brawl and got both players ejected, but the sight of the quiet Parish unloading a forearm to the face of Laimbeer as the two battled for a rebound showed how much antagonism existed between the teams.

Detroit would break through the next season for the first of its three straight NBA Finals appearances, falling to the Lakers in seven games. But the Pistons would win the next two titles, setting the tone of physical play that would permeate throughout the Eastern Conference in the 1990s.

The NBA Draft Lottery

After the Rockets selected Olajuwon with the first pick in 1984, there continued to be outcry that teams were tanking to make sure they could be one of the top two picks and part of the coin flip to determine who won the No. 1 overall pick. Commissioner David Stern then changed the method of the draft order to a full-fledged lottery in which every non-playoff team had an equal chance of securing the No. 1 overall pick.

The 1985 draft turned into great theater since Georgetown center Patrick Ewing was clearly the best player available to be selected and would be a cornerstone in any franchise. The event instantly became must-see television for all NBA fans, and the conspiracy theorists of sport instantly cried foul when the New York Knicks won the first draft lottery and selected Ewing. From frozen envelopes to dented corners of envelopes, there are still people who believe the first NBA draft lottery was rigged to help the team in the biggest media market.

Since then, the NBA has come up with tweaks to protect teams with the worst record from falling too far down the draft board since there are now 14 non-playoff teams every year. But it sometimes can't be helped when these struggling teams trade away picks years in advance and it winds up with good teams having the top pick… like the Boston Celtics do this summer after reaching the Eastern Conference finals.

Cleveland… still a mistake by the lake

There was little good news in the world of sports in Cleveland in the 1980s – the Indians never finished above fifth place the entire decade, the Browns lost to the Broncos three times in a four-year span in the AFC title game, but the Cavaliers were their own unique brand of futility tanks to the ineptitude of owner Ted Stepien.

From the 1980-81 through the 1983-84 seasons, the Cavaliers never won more than 28 games, in large part due to Stepien's bumbling. He alienated the community with disparaging remarks against the African-American community and was vilified by the team's remaining fans when he ran play-by-play announcer Joe Tait out of town.

But what set Stepien apart from other meddlesome owners was the team's propensity to trade away first-round picks. In the two-plus seasons Stepien owned the team from 1980-82, the Cavaliers dealt five first-round picks, including three to the expansion Dallas Mavericks. It got to the point where the league had to step in and pass what became known as the "Stepien Rule" in which restricted teams from trading first-round picks in consecutive years.

And those decisions crippled the franchise for more than a decade. They dealt away their top pick in 1982, which turned out to be the No. 1 pick overall. The Lakers used that on James Worthy. The following year, the Mavericks took Derek Harper with the 11th overall pick they acquired from Cleveland.

In 1984, the Cavs would have had the fourth overall pick, which the Mavericks used on Sam Perkins. Other options that year included Auburn forward Charles Barkley and Gonzaga point guard John Stockton. The Cavaliers selected center Tim McCormick 12th that year, a compensation pick provided by the league to help overcome Stepien's mistakes, but they promptly dealt him to Seattle.

His last deal with the Mavericks that gave Dallas a first-round pick in 1986 turned out to be center Roy Tarpley.

The Nuggets' Talented Trio

While the Lakers and Rockets dominated the headlines in the early 1980s, there were some other good teams in the Western Conference. One was the Denver Nuggets, coached by Doug Moe. The former ABA guard developed a high-tempo offense that didn't seem to operate on any set of principles aside from moving the ball quickly and shoot even quicker.

It also helped Moe had three standout players in Dan Issel, Alex English and Kiki Vandeweghe. Issel, nicknamed "The Horse" for his durability, was a holdover from the ABA days and could still score with anyone regardless of league. The ABA's all-time leading scorer averaged at least 21.6 points in five straight seasons for the Nuggets while making the playoffs every year.

English was originally a second-round pick by the Bucks in 1976 and didn't blossom until the Nuggets acquired him in a trade from Indiana during the 1979-80 season. He averaged at least 23.8 points in his next nine seasons in Denver, earning honors as the top scorer in the NBA for the 1980s, and his 25,613 career points rank 17th all-time.

VanDeWeghe was originally selected 11th by the Mavericks in 1980, but forced a trade to Denver by December. His three full seasons with the Nuggets were incredibly proficient as he averaged 21.5, 26.7 and 29.4 points. His career high of 51 points came in the NBA's highest-scoring game of all-time, a 186-184 triple-overtime loss to the Detroit Pistons.

In a three-season stretch from 1981-84, the Nuggets averaged 124.5 points behind the trio. However, their lack of defense meant they also allowed 124.5 points per game as they outscored opponents by just four points over those 246 contests while going 129-117.

The Woeful San Diego Clippers

Despite his best efforts, Stepien did not have a monopoly on ineptitude at the ownership level. While Donald Sterling gained worldwide notoriety for his racist comments in 2014, he was sowing the seeds of misery in the Clippers franchise as a fledgling owner in the 1980s. He bought the team in 1981 for the paltry sum of $12.5 million with promises of making the team into a contender.

You couldn't go anywhere in San Diego without seeing Sterling's face on a bus or a billboard. But while his friend Jerry Buss instantly turned the Lakers into a contender, Sterling was left with a sagging Clippers franchise that didn't have a winning record throughout the decade.

The NBA fined him when he publicly said it would be OK if his team would finish last for a better chance to select Sampson with the first pick in the 1983 draft. His love affair with moving the team to Los Angeles began in 1982, and an investigation by his fellow owners resulted in a recommendation to terminate him as an owner due to late payments to creditors and players.

But the following year, then-vice president David Stern suggested to Sterling he let Alan Rothenberg – the eventual savior of soccer in the United States – to take over the day-to-day duties of the team. Sterling relented, and the palace coup wouldn't take place for another three decades.

Random Facts and Figures

1. The 1985-86 Bulls finished 30-52 and still qualified for the playoffs. It remains the worst postseason qualifying record in NBA history.

2. Jordan's 63-point game stands out for a few reasons. One is that he didn't attempt a 3-pointer. In fact, the Bulls only took two in 102 shots for the game. Two is that Jordan was a very good free throw shooter. He sank 19 of 21 from the line in that game. And third, despite taking 41 shots from the field, he also led the team with six assists.

3. The Lakers' Game 7 victory in 1988 was their first in the finals since moving to Los Angeles in 1960. They had lost the previous five decisive games since winning the title in 1954 while located in Minneapolis.

4. In VanDeWeghe's 51-point game, he combined with English and Issel for 126 of the team's 184 points on 50 of 78 shooting. The Pistons had a potent trio of their own as Thomas, Kelly Tripucka and John Long accounted for 123 points while making 50 of 84 shots from the field. The game was tied at 145 at the end of regulation.

5. Magic Johnson far and away had the most assists in the 1980s with 8,369. Thomas was a distant second with 6,985.

6. Like Jordan, it took some time for Ewing to have a winning season. The Knicks won only 47 games in his first two seasons and then made the playoffs in

1988 despite finish 38-44. They finally broke through the following season, the second and last under Rick Pitino, going 52-30 and reaching the second round before Pitino left to resurrect the University of Kentucky.

7. For all of Bird's prowess from 3-point range, the Celtics never used it as a primary weapon. Bird finished sixth in the 1980s with 462 3-pointers made – even one-time teammate Danny Ainge had more (514).

8. Philadelphia 76ers guard Maurice Cheeks had nearly as many defensive rebounds (1,731) as he did steals (1,709) in the 1980s.

9. Jordan finished 15th in points scored in the 1980s with 14,016 despite playing only 427 games. Every other player in the top 25 in scoring played at least 597 games.

10. All told, six players were given one-year bans for cocaine use in the 1980s. They were: John Drew, Micheal Ray Richardson, Lewis Lloyd, Mitchell Wiggins, Duane Washington and Chris Washburn. Richardson, Wiggins and Washburn were all first-round picks, and Richardson and Washburn went fourth and third overall, respectively.

11. It may be one of the closest things to an unassailable record in NBA history – Magic Johnson has 2,346 postseason assists, 507 more than second-place John Stockton. Heading into the 2017 NBA Finals, LeBron James is third with 1,439.

12. Five different players had 60-point games in the 1980s, paced by Jordan's 69. The others were Karl Malone, Bird, Tom Chambers and Bernard King.

13. There continues to be debate over whether Thomas "froze out" Jordan during the 1985 All-Star game. It was Jordan's first All-Star game and veteran players were reportedly upset over Jordan's flashy ways. While both Jordan and Thomas downplayed the talk, Johnson said it did happen in a book he co-wrote with Bird and Jackie MacMullan called "When the Game was Ours."

14. How bad were the Clippers in the 1980s? Despite losing in the 1987 NBA Finals, the Celtics still had more wins that postseason (13) than the Clippers did in the 1986-87 regular season (12).

15. David Robinson didn't arrive in San Antonio until the 1989-90 season, but his impact was instant. The Spurs improved 35 games in the win column from 21 to 56 and won their first Division title since 1983.

TRIVIA TIME

1. How many NBA Finals appearances did the Lakers make from 1980-81 to 1989-90?

    A. 5
    B. 7
    C. 6
    D. 8

2. Adrian Dantley ended his playing career in which team?

    A. Buffalo Braves
    B. Utah Jazz
    C. Milwaukee Bucks
    D. Detroit Pistons

3. True or False: The Boston Celtics won at least 50 games every season during the 1980s?

4. Because of the Celtics and the 76ers, the Milwaukee Bucks were one of the best Eastern Conference teams of the 1980s no one remembers. How many consecutive Central Division titles did they win that decade?

A.   3
B.   5
C.   4
D.   6

6.   In 1980-81, the expansion Dallas Mavericks began
their first NBA season. Who was their leading
average scorer?

A.   Brad Davis
B.   Jim Spanarkel
C.   Geoff Huston
D.   Tom LaGarde

Answers:

1-B

2- C

3-False, the Celtics went 42-40 in 1988-89.

4-D

5-C.

Don't forget to have the second part of the book!